Riding Back in Time

On My Daddy's Harley-Davidson

Illustrations by
Julie Bauknecht

Jean Davidson & Jon Davidson Oeflein

Text © 2006 Jean Davidson
Illustrations © 2006 Julie Bauknecht

Published by The Guest Cottage
"The Home of Good Reading"™
PO Box 848, Woodruff, WI 54568
www.theguestcottage.com
1-800-333-8122

The
Guest
Cottage
"The Home of Good Reading"

ISBN 978-1-930596-47-4

Designed by Patricia Bickner Linder
anewleaf-books.com

Library of Congress Cataloging-in-Publication Data

Davidson, Jean, 1937-
  Riding back in time / Jean Davidson & her son, Jon Davidson Oeflein ;
illustrated by Julie Bauknecht.
      p. cm.
  ISBN 1-930596-47-2 (hardcover)
  1. Motorcycles--History--Juvenile literature. 2. Davidson, Jean,
1937---Childhood and youth--Juvenile literature. I. Oeflein, Jon Davidson.
II. Bauknecht, Julie, ill. III. Title.
  TL440.15.D38 2005
  629.227'109--dc22
                              2005030139

Printed in China

To Nic, Carter, Max, Ryder, Nicole, Annie,
Natalie, and all children …
You each have a special gift. Find it, develop it,
and share your uniqueness with the world!
—J.D. & J.D.O.

Dedicated to my little helpers,
Michalie, Mackenzie and Madilyn
—J.B.

Daddy . . . That was a fun ride!
I love motorcycles! You make lots of
motorcycles at your factory. I know
you learned to make motorcycles from your
daddy.

But . . .
Who taught him how to make motorcycles?
Did Grandpa invent motorcycles? What did
people do before motorcycles?

Oh, Jeannie … you are so full of questions! You ask so many for such a young girl. Do you want me to tell you the whole story of where motorcycles came from?

Yes … yes … Please tell me!

Okay, I'll tell you the whole story.

Oh, that sounds fun! I'll listen AND pretend I'm a little girl way back in time!

It all started a long, long time ago way back in the year 3500 B.C. in a country called Sumeria. That's more than 5,000 years ago!

Somebody, nobody knows exactly who, made the first wheel. It was made of wood and was very heavy.

Some wheels were made of stone and they were REALLY heavy.

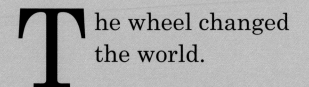

T he wheel changed the world.

People started to put wheels on everything from wagons in 2000 B.C. ...

I'd rather be hauling my bones than you guys.

Oh, brother!

... to chariots in 1000 B.C.

In the late 1700s, the early beginnings of the bicycle appeared.

In England, which is across the ocean from us, the velocipede was made.

It had two wheels and you pushed with your legs. Many people called it a boneshaker because of its rough ride.

You need strong legs!

And good balance!

SSSStrenuous.

Then in 1839, a Mr. MacMillan, who was a blacksmith in Scotland, added treadles to a velocipede. This led to the making of the modern bicycle.

Do you remember me telling you that your grandfather's mom and dad came from Scotland? You have Scottish heritage.

For the remainder of the 1800s, bicycles took many forms.

The Penny-Farthing was very popular. It had a large front wheel and a small back wheel and it was hard to climb up on. You needed long legs to reach the pedals.

It's a long way to the ground.

SSSScary!

If you crash forward, it's called a header.

Daddy, I want to talk about motorcycles!

Jeannie, I know you want to talk about motorcycles, but to get there we first have to talk about STEAM!

Like the wheel, steam changed the world.

Back in the late 1600s, people discovered that heating water and changing it into steam created a powerful force.

In 1765, another man from Scotland, named James Watt, used this to develop a really great steam engine.

How hot would water have to be to change into steam?

212 degrees— that's boiling!

Steam engines began
powering everything
from trains . . .

Choo . . . choo!

... to riverboats. Now people could get places faster and easier than ever before.

Now that we have people riding bicycles
and powerful steam engines working away,
we are ready to talk about …

MOTORCYCLES!

In 1869, two brothers from France
put a steam engine on a bicycle
and got the whole thing going …

I wouldn't sit
on a steam
engine.

My legs might
get cooked.

But, steam engines had lots of problems. People started to look for a different fuel for their motors.

They looked down, down, down into the earth ... and what did they find?

OIL!

Whee!

It's raining!

Scientists learned that oil from the earth could be turned into gasoline. The gasoline could be ignited to release another great force.
Just like steam, this force could be used to power an engine.

It was called an internal combustion engine. Soon, it replaced many steam engines because it could be made much smaller and was not as dangerous.

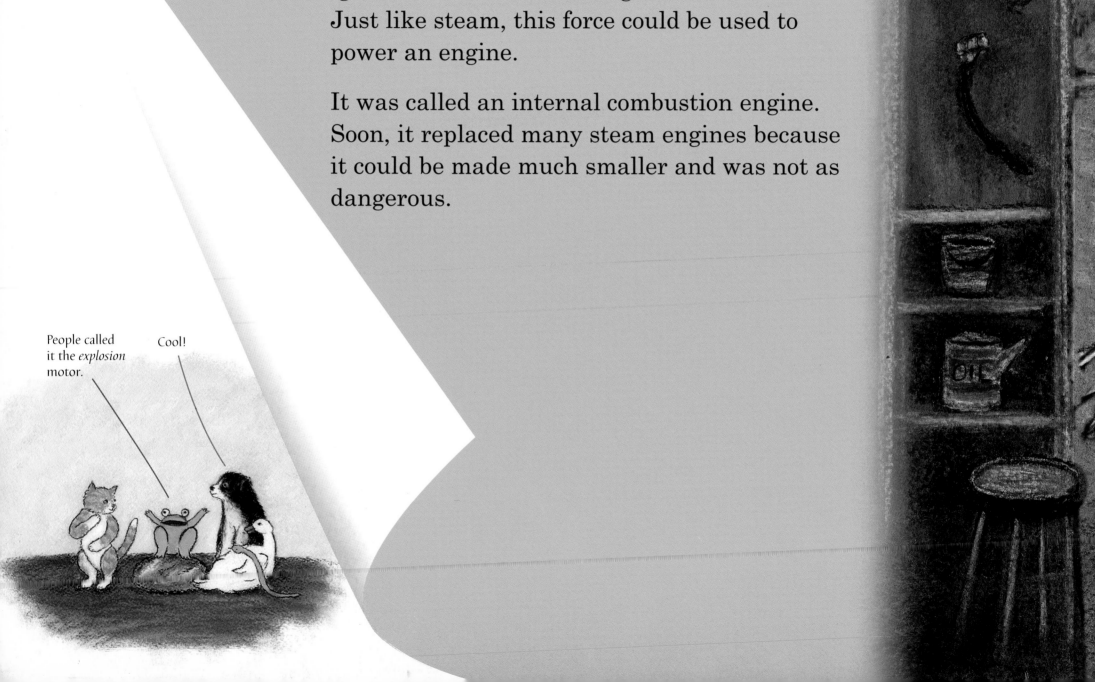

People called it the *explosion* motor.

Cool!

In 1885, Gottlieb Daimler put his gas engine on a wooden bicycle. It didn't go much faster than you could walk, but it opened the doors to the future.

Soon, many people wanted to
put a motor on a bicycle.

One big problem was where
to put the motor. Everyone
had a different idea.

Your grandfather, Walter Davidson, with his brothers, William and Arthur, and their best friend, William Harley, had an idea. They decided that the best place for the motor was as low as possible between the wheels. They used this idea to build the first Harley-Davidson motorcycle. It didn't work very well, so they kept making it better.

Finally, in 1903, they made one they thought was good enough to show the world.

Many other people made motorcycles,
but only Harley-Davidson has stayed
in business for over 100 years.

Walter, William and Arthur Davidson
and William Harley are gone now,
but their motorcycles live on.

VIDSON
William Davidson
Walter Davidson
Arthur Davidson
William Harley
WAGON
CHARIOT
VELOCIPEDE
PENNY-FARTHING
STEAM ENGINE
TRAIN
RIVERBOAT
BICYCLE
MOTORCYCLE
STEAM BICYCLE

Jeannie, remember . . .

Nothing great is accomplished without people working together.

Your grandfather had his brothers and their best friend. By working together as a team and using the discoveries of past inventors, they began making the Harley-Davidson motorcycles that everyone still loves today.

Go Team! SSSStupendous!

Daddy, Grandpa sure was special.

Yes, but I know some-one else special.

Who?

YOU! Now jump on and let's ride home!

the *Best Motorcycle in the Whole Wide World* Jean tells the stories of how Harley-Davidson started and the fun she had as a little girl.

Riding Back in Time on My Daddy's Harley-Davidson is Jean's second children's book. Jean and her son Jon share what discoveries and inventions needed to happen in the world before the making of the Harley-Davidson motorcycle. Jeannie is an eight-year-old girl who gets to pretend what it was like going back in time. This book is a delightful way for children to learn the history of transportation and how it led up to the making of the Harley-Davidson motorcycle which is loved all over the world.

Jean lives in Milwaukee, Wisconsin, and can be reached at: www.jeandavidson.com or email jean@jeandavidson.com.

About the Authors

JEAN DAVIDSON is an internationally known author and speaker. She is the granddaughter of Walter Davidson, one of the founders and first president of Harley-Davidson Motor Company. Her father, Gordon Davidson, was the vice president of manufacturing. She has written three previous books, *Growing Up Harley-Davidson, Jean Davidson's Harley-Davidson Family Album*, and *My Daddy Makes the Best Motorcycle in the Whole Wide World*. These books are being enjoyed by readers through out the world. Jean travels extensively speaking about the personal stories of the Harley-Davidson Motorcycle legacy. In her first children's book, *My Daddy Makes*

JON DAVIDSON OEFLEIN lives in Wisconsin with his wife and their two sons. He is an antique motorcycle enthusiast who restores and rides classic Harley-Davidsons. Jon and his siblings share and maintain a motorcycle and memorabilia collection that their father started many decades ago. Jon loves to spend his time riding on the same roads his great grandfather, Walter Davidson, and his grandfather, Gordon Davidson, rode on as they built the Harley-Davidson Motor Company. Jon hosts, and can be reached through, his website www.suicideshifters.com that caters to fans of antique motorcycles. Jon would like to thank his mother for collaborating with him on this fun book and his father for passing on the love of classic bikes to him.

Pictured above left is Jon's 1946 H-D G that he restored with the help of good friends Anthony Jankoski, and Lance and Drew Marshall.

About the Illustrator

JULIE BAUKNECHT has loved to draw and paint as long as she can remember. She believes you should live life to the fullest and love what you do. Julie presently lives in Antigo, Wisconsin, with her husband and three children. She can be reached at JulieBauknecht@verizon.net or www.JulieBauknecht.com